S FLAG

by Susan Rose Simms

Cody Koala

An Imprint of Pop!
popbooksonline.com

abdopublishing.com
Published by Pop!, a division of ABDO, PO Box 398166, Minneapolis,
Minnesota 55439. Copyright © 2019 by POP, LLC. International copyrights
reserved in all countries. No part of this book may be reproduced in any
form without written permission from the publisher. Pop!™ is a trademark
and logo of POP, LLC.

Printed in the United States of America, North Mankato, Minnesota

042018
092018

♻ THIS BOOK CONTAINS
RECYCLED MATERIALS

Cover Photo: Shutterstock Images
Interior Photos: Shutterstock Images, 1, 5, 8, 11 (top left), 11 (top right), 11
(bottom right), 13 (bottom left), 13 (bottom right), 13 (top), 17, 20–21; North
Wind Picture Archives, 7; iStockphoto, 11 (bottom left), 18; JSC/NASA, 14

Editor: Meg Gaertner
Series Designer: Laura Mitchell

Library of Congress Control Number: 2017963471
Publisher's Cataloging-in-Publication Data
Names: Simms, Susan Rose, author.
Title: The US flag / by Susan Rose Simms.
Description: Minneapolis, Minnesota : Pop!, 2019. | Series: US symbols |
    Includes online resources and index.
Identifiers: ISBN 9781532160493 (lib.bdg.) | ISBN 9781532161612 (ebook) |
Subjects: LCSH: Flags--United States--Juvenile literature. | Signs and
    symbols--United States--Juvenile literature. | Emblems, National--
    Juvenile literature.
Classification: DDC 929.920--dc23

Hello! My name is

Cody Koala

Pop open this book and you'll find QR codes like this one, loaded with information, so you can learn even more!

Scan this code* and others like it while you read,

or visit the website below to make this book pop.

popbooksonline.com/the-us-flag

*Scanning QR codes requires a web-enabled smart device with a QR code reader app and a camera.

Table of Contents

The US Flag

Each country has a national flag. The US flag has 13 red or white stripes. Fifty stars sit on a blue background. The US flag did not always look this way.

The US flag is also called Old Glory.

Watch a video here!

History of the Flag

The US government passed the first Flag Act in 1777. The new law created the **official** flag for the United States.

Learn more here!

The first flag had only 13 stars. At the time, the United States was made up of 13 states. Every time a new state joined the United States, the government added a star to the flag.

The current flag is the 27th US flag. It was made in 1960 after Hawaii became a state.

1795
(15 stars)

1822
(24 stars)

1861
(33 stars)

1960
(50 stars)

Chapter 3

Red, White, and Blue

The flag's 13 stripes stand for the original 13 states. The 50 stars stand for the 50 states in the United States.

Complete an activity here!

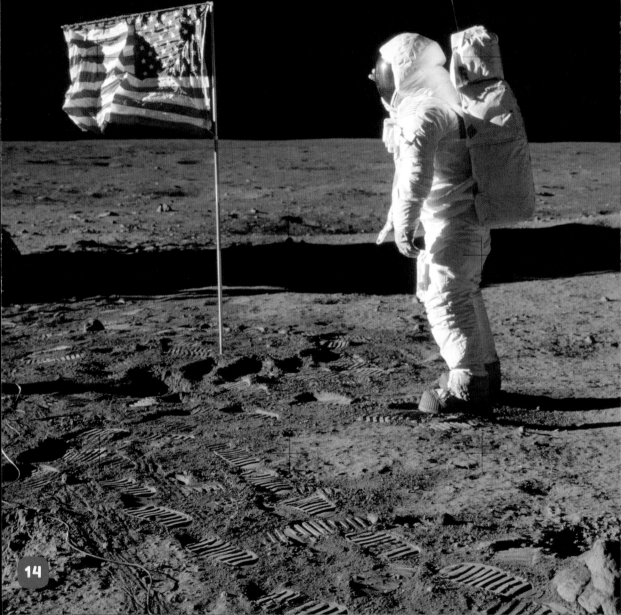

Seven stripes are red.

The red stands for bravery.

Six stripes are white.

The white stands for **innocence**. The blue color stands for **justice**.

Neil Armstrong brought the US flag to the moon in 1969.

Chapter 4

Pledge of Allegiance

The flag blowing in the wind is a beautiful sight. It **inspired** Francis Bellamy to write the **Pledge** of **Allegiance**.

Learn more here!

People often say the Pledge of Allegiance in schools. They place their right hand over their heart when they say it. This shows **respect**.

The Pledge of Allegiance
says the flag stands for
freedom and justice.

The US flag reminds
Americans to be proud of
their country.

Making Connections

Text-to-Self

Do you say the Pledge of Allegiance at your school? What does the pledge mean to you?

Text-to-Text

What other US symbols have you read about? What do they stand for?

Text-to-World

Where do you see the US flag? How do people honor the flag?

Glossary

allegiance – loyal support.

innocence – free from guilt or evil.

inspired – filled with a powerful feeling.

justice – treating people fairly and equally.

official – approved by someone in charge.

pledge – to make a promise.

respect – having a high opinion of someone or something.

Index

Online Resources

popbooksonline.com

Thanks for reading this Cody Koala book!

Scan this code* and others like it in this book, or visit the website below to make this book pop!

popbooksonline.com/the-us-flag

*Scanning QR codes requires a web-enabled smart device with a QR code reader app and a camera.